A GRACE-FILLED JOURNEY HOME

A GRACE-FILLED JOURNEY HOME

Stan Jacobson

EMMAUS JOURNEY PUBLISHING, LLC
Algona, Wahington

Copyright © 2015 by Stan Jacobson

All rights reserved. No part of this book may be reproduced, stored in a retrieval system, or transmitted, in any form or by any means, electronic, mechanical, photocopying, recording or otherwise, without the written permission of the Publisher. Published in the United States by Emmaus Journey Publishing, LLC

ISBN-13: 9781518654374
ISBN-10: 1518654371

Cover photo by Andrew K Jacobson

All bible quotations are taken from the New Revised Standard Version

Library of Congress Control Number: 2015917264
CreateSpace Independent Publishing Platform,
North Charleston, South Carolina

DEDICATION

Diane Marie, or as she was known in Mexico, Diana Maria, was my soulmate, my life partner with whom I intended to grow old. It is to Diane that I owe the writing of this book and even my life.

PREFACE

Teilhard de Chardin wrote the following admonition in "Trust in the Slow Work of God":

Above all, trust in the slow work of God.
We are quite naturally impatient in every-
    thing to reach the end without delay.
We should like to skip the intermediate
    stages.
We are impatient of being on the way
    to something unknown, something new.
And, yet, it is the law of all progress that
    it is made by passing through some
    stages of instability—
    and that it may take a very long time.

And so I think it is with you; your ideas
    mature gradually—
    let them grow, let them shape
    themselves without undue haste.
Don't try to force them on, as though
    you could be today what time
    (that is to say, grace and circumstances
    acting on your own good will)
    will make you tomorrow.

> Only God could say what this new spirit
>   gradually forming within you will be.
> Give our Lord the benefit of believing
>   that God's hand is leading you,
> And accept the anxiety of feeling yourself
>   in suspense
>   and incomplete.

I have found that this slow work of God in my life has involved so many people, family and friends. The members of First Lutheran Church, Volga, South Dakota; Trinity Lutheran Church, Endicott, Washington; Immanuel Lutheran Church, Everson, Washington; and Grace Lutheran Church, Des Moines, Washington, have been instrumental in God's formation of my life, and God's Spirit has used them to help form my intentions for my aging years.

This book of letters would have ended up with all my other journals on my shelves gathering dust were it not for the help and encouragement of my editor, Jean Gilbertson. Also, Darlene Malmo, David Head, Doug Anderson, and Carol Ervin were significantly helpful in previewing and critiquing the rough draft of *A Grace-Filled Journey Home*. Kristi Kath constantly helped me when my ineptness with the computer caused me to go further bald. My journey of life as well as my journey of writing is possible only because of the input and the encouragement of others. Thank you to each.

As I began this journey of writing, my intention was to spend all my aging years with my wife, Diane. I am who I am today because of her love, her ability to see the positive in me when I was not, and her encouragement of me to write and keep on writing. Also, my sons, Andrew and Peter, will continue to be my support, even as I continue to age.

All scriptural references used in the book are from The New Revised Standard Version (NRSV).

INTRODUCTION

The year was 1986. The event was a graduation dinner for the members of a graduate program in Marriage and Family Therapy. Dr. Doug Anderson, the director of the program and of Presbyterian Counseling Services in Seattle, Washington, gave very descriptive remarks about each of the dozen or so graduate students.

It was my turn. What would he say? How would he describe me? He put a small backpack on my shoulders and proclaimed me to be a "hobo." Hum, not very flattering, I thought. What in the world does that mean? He went on to say that he saw me as a person who was on a life-long journey, a life-long spiritual journey in which I would always be traveling by seeking, by learning. Since that time the word *journey* has been an important self-descriptive marker for my life.

This writing journey began nearly five years ago, September 2010, in the offices of Grace Lutheran Church in Des Moines, Washington. Carol and Kristi, at that time the church's faithful office manager and administrative assistant, and I were talking about our experiences with our aging parents, or, in my case, with my aging mother-in-law. In all seriousness we promised each other that when we get older we will not be as stubborn as those for whom we were caring. I commented how I wanted to sit down and write myself a letter to remind myself in the years to come of my good intentions. Thus began my writing journey of "A Grace-Filled Journey Home."

STAN JACOBSON

This book is a series of letters written to myself highlighting my positive intentions as I grow older and eventually face my mortality. As I write this introduction, I will be sixty-eight years young in three months, and I have commissioned both of my sons to "encourage" me, "make me" read these letters on or around each of my forthcoming birthdays. In this way, I will remember these positive intentions, and I hope to live them as well as remember them.

I asked a friend of mine to read a few of the letters and offer a critique. Subsequently, she described them as more "psychological, self-help" ideas. My heart sank a little, for "self-help" is not the objective of this writing. These letters originate from over thirty years of pastoral encounters and other lively relationships with the aging. They are the important lessons that I personally want to remember as the years lengthen and mortality keeps creeping closer.

I have seen many gray-haired ladies and gentlemen face their aging gracefully, and an equal number have virtually been hell for those who have had to care for them. In the future, I want to remember what my positive intentions are for myself as I grow older and eventually face my mortality. I have encountered tremendous models of grace and virtue but I have also ministered to those who make life miserable for all who enter their rooms or who offer a friendly phone call.

Oh, how I want my later years to be full of grace and thanksgiving. I want them to be gifts to my family and friends and, therefore, I am writing myself a series of letters to help me remember those intentions and lessons learned on this journey to gray hair and flabby muscles, but treasured memories.

I have walked through "the valley of the shadow of death" with friends, parishioners, and family. I have been a shepherd, a spiritual guide, and I have walked alongside those who have grown old with me. In this journey of life, God's Spirit has been my teacher and has used so many people—Bill and Joan, Cal and Martha—the list is too long to number. All these fellow pilgrims have faced their aging and have faced their mortality in a variety of ways. I have learned from them how to live, act, think, and relate to others as the years fly by.

As I embarked on writing these letters, my wife, Diane, and I were the caregivers for Hazelle, my mother-in-law. Then in June 2013 my world was forever altered. First, Hazelle passed from this life into an eternal realm of glory. One week later Diane was diagnosed with Stage IV non-small cell lung cancer and thirteen months later she too died. My life changed as did the writing of these letters. Readers will notice the change in tone.

Furthermore, many of the letters have a postscript added. These postscripts seek to give Biblical expansion to the theme of the letter or to add the thoughts and comments of other authors.

So, even as I hope to read and remember in the future these lessons from my past, so I hope and pray that each of you will also ponder your aging process and make your journey home one of grace, living and aging well.

CONTENTS

Preface..vii
Introduction..ix
Letter 1   "I Want to Sit Down and Write Myself a Letter"......... 1
Letter 2   "Stubborn Independence"............................... 4
Letter 3   "True Identity"....................................... 7
Letter 4   "Surrendering My Mind"................................ 9
Letter 5   "Journey"..12
Letter 6   "Aging as Our Teacher"...............................15
Letter 7   "Aging as Our Teacher: Part 2".......................17
Letter 8   "Positive Attitude/Be Grateful"..................... 20
Letter 9   "Life Doesn't Center in Pills"......................23
Letter 10 "Premature Death"...................................25
Letter 11 "Don't Postpone Living".............................27
Letter 12 "Clutter"... 30
Letter 13 "Take Time to Listen"...............................32
Letter 14 "Self-Absorption / Fan the Flames of Love".......... 34
Letter 15 "Stay Active"....................................... 36
Letter 16 "Signs of Hope".....................................38
Letter 17 "Final Blessings"................................... 40
Letter 18 "Give Chocolate".................................... 42
Letter 19 "Mountains Climbed from a Wheelchair"............... 44
Letter 20 "Memories"..47
Letter 21 "Utter Darkness"....................................49
Letter 22 "When?"...53

Letter 23	"Wisdom of the Aged"	55
Letter 24	"Family History"	58
Letter 25	"Facing Death"	60
Letter 26	"The End / The Beginning, for Both of Us"	63
Letter 27	"A Physical Reminder"	65
Letter 28	"The Other Half of the Story"	67
Letter 29	"Vulnerable to the End"	69
Letter 30	"Beauty"	71

1

"I WANT TO SIT DOWN AND WRITE MYSELF A LETTER"

September 28, 2010

Dear Stan,

Perhaps I am putting into print what no one wants to ever read, let alone think about. For it might be that you will not know who it is that is writing to you. It might be that the writer of this letter is as strange to you as are all those who enter your sterile room. But my hope and prayer are that this letter and all those that follow will bring a smile to your face, a beat to your heart, and an energetic kick to your aging mind, for, you see, the writer of this letter is you. That's right!

Stan, you are writing to yourself, and if you, the reader, is not Stan, you are not intruding on private letters, but you are reading the rambling thoughts of one who daily is getting older, but still has a mind that is for the most part alert and lucid.

At this point, I want to write to myself, because what I have seen and have heard through countless pastoral encounters and other lively relationships with the aging has shown me important lessons that I want to remember as the years lengthen and mortality keeps creeping forward.

Stan, first of all, who are you? Oh, how I hope you remember, but just a quick sketch. You are, above all else, a child of God, baptized as an infant, called already in your mother's womb to be a servant of God. Your mother, Helen, and father, Nestor, were in their middle-forties when you were conceived as a "mistake." A few years before she died, when you were in your early twenties, your mother told you that after you were conceived she was ashamed and hid from the public eye. She felt too old to have a child.

She must have forgotten her pedigree in the long line of elderly women in the scriptures who conceived in their "golden years." But something happened. God gave her a gift, a gift that subsequently has become significant to you, her son by "mistake." God's Word came to her. God "spoke" to my mother in her pregnancy and she was given the assurance that this child, kicking and punching in her womb, was to be a child of God, used as a servant of God in this world. That is who you are, a child of God, a servant of God.

Yes, I hope these letters will trigger aspects of your spiritual journey that will enable you to continue to be a "light," "listening ear," and "the hand of God" to others.

These letters come out of specific conversations with people as well as my pondering of my own aging process. I hope to never forget these lessons, lest I become "a pain in the rear" to those who are caring for me.

So, Stan, read and remember, live and age, and even die gracefully by living in His undying love.

Yours,

PS   There are many theological understandings of baptism and when and how God comes to us and makes us children of God. Jeremiah wrote, "Now the word of the LORD came to me saying, 'Before I formed you in the womb I knew you, and before you were born I consecrated you; I appointed you a prophet to the nations'" (Jeremiah 1:4-5).

Even the Apostle Paul, who had a life-altering encounter with the living Christ on the road to Damascus, claimed that God knew him before he was born. "But when God, who had set me apart before I was born and called me through his grace, was pleased to reveal his Son to me ..." (Galatians 1:15–16a).

I do not place myself on the spiritual level of these giants of the faith, but I do claim God's call upon my life from my mother's womb, and I cannot remember a time in my life when I did not know, on a very deep level, that I was loved and claimed by God. Thus, for me, life has not been a search for my true identity, trying to find out who I am, but rather it has always been a *becoming, a growing into* who God called me to be.

2

"STUBBORN INDEPENDENCE"

October 1, 2010

Dear Stan,

As I described in the Introduction, the idea of these letters came to me one day as I was visiting with Carol and Kristi in the office of Grace Lutheran Church, Des Moines, Washington. We were talking about our experiences with our aging parents or, in my case, with my aging mother-in-law.

We said that when we get older we will not be as stubborn, but we will listen to the advice of our loved ones. I commented how I wanted to sit down and write myself a letter to remind myself in the years to come of my good intentions. So here are the letters.

Stubborn? Oh, I'm not stubborn *now*, at least I don't think I am. Diane (my wife) would disagree, maybe. But somehow it seems that as people age they get over-saturated with this negative quality.

The Scriptures have a lot to say about stubbornness. Not least is Psalm 81:12, "So I gave them over to their stubborn hearts, to follow their own counsels."

Also, 1 Samuel 15:23a reads, "For rebellion is no less a sin than divination, and stubbornness is like iniquity and idolatry." Stubbornness seems to indicate that a person thinks he or she is wiser than others and even God, and so we place ourselves above God.

One of the primary areas where stubbornness is expressed is in one's desire to remain independent after aging has made independence unwise. Some seniors stay in their homes far too long, drive beyond the time of safe driving, or handle finances or even medication beyond the time of reasonableness.

I want to remember that this stubborn insistence upon independence can be both very dangerous to myself and to others and very annoying to those who desire my best welfare. Perhaps what I need to remember is that even now, at the ripe young age of sixty-three, there is no such thing as independence, but rather an interdependence with others and a total dependence upon my Lord and God.

I want to remind myself that absolute independence is an illusion and that family and community mean we are interdependent. People need people. Family needs family.

As I age I will need people even more than now and to hold on to my stubbornness will only cause friction and needless difficulties. There is no need to stubbornly hold on to things or patterns as in the past. That is not what life is about.

So, Stan, read and remember, live and age, and even die gracefully by living in His freeing love.

Yours,

PS   We live in a culture that prizes individualism whereas many other cultures, especially African cultures, have a different understanding of the meaning of personhood. Archbishop Desmond Tutu in *No Future Without Forgiveness* wrote about *Ubuntu*, which is an African understanding of the essence of personhood. Instead of a strong sense of independence, the African culture stresses the concept that "a person is a person through other persons," thus there is an interdependence rather than isolation and independence. Bishop Tutu describes *Ubuntu* by saying, "I am human because I belong. I participate, I share" (p. 31).

3

"TRUE IDENTITY"

October 2, 2010

Dear Stan,

Sometimes I ponder, "What is important for me to remember in the future years? What will I remember?" Perhaps I will remember stories. At least I want to remember *this* story.

In my internship year at seminary, I entered a hospital room where an elderly pastor was lying in Bed 1, crying: "I'm nobody now! I cannot do anything! I'm nobody!" He had been a pastor, and even in his aging years he had visited countless people in the hospital, but now it was his time. He lay in a hospital bed, recovering from a major heart attack, but his heart was attacked by more than clogged arteries. He was crying in pain from the suffocating calcium of a false identity. He saw his identity simply by what he could do, and now that his "doing" was amputated, so was his identity. He had no identity as a "being," but only as a "doer."

Stan, remember who you are: **A Child of God!** Long before you became a pastor and long after your retirement, you were, you are, and you will be **A Child**

of God. You are loved and forgiven. You are a person of worth, not because of what you can do, but because of who and whose you are. Remember what the Scriptures have to say to you, "See what love the Father has given us, that we should be called children of God; and that is what we are" (1 John 3:1a).

So, Stan, read and remember, and live and age, and even die gracefully by remembering that you are loved, you are forgiven.

Yours,

PS   Tullian Tchividjian in *One Way Love* quotes Paul Zahl:

> "Grace is love that seeks you out when you have nothing to give in return. Grace is love coming at you that has nothing to do with you. Grace is being loved when you are unlovable. ... The cliché definition of grace is "unconditional love." It is a true cliché, for it is a good description of the thing ...
>
> "Let's go a little further, though. Grace is a love that has nothing to do with you, the beloved. It has everything and only to do with the lover. Grace is irrational in the sense that it has nothing to do with weights and measures. It has nothing to do with my intrinsic qualities or so-called "gifts" (whatever they may be). It reflects a decision on the part of the giver, the one who loves, in relation to the receiver, the one who is loved, that negates any qualifications the receiver may personally hold ...
>
> Grace is *one-way love*" (p. 32f).

When our worth and value are intricately interwoven with what we *do,* then when we are no longer able to accomplish or perform, we become worthless in our own eyes. But the fact is, we are made worthy by the One who loves us, who gave His only Son for us. We are loved into worthiness. We are loved into value. We are loved and, therefore, each of us is God's child.

4

"SURRENDERING MY MIND"

October 15, 2010

Dear Stan,

There are moments that really scare me even now. There are times I cannot remember a name, a fact, a word, or even an experience, and I wonder if this is "the beginning." Those scary words "dementia" and "Alzheimer's disease" invade my thoughts. Of course, I hope these lapses of memory are simply natural progressions of aging and not the enemy of disease attacking with brutal force. But if it is, how do I want to face this onslaught? Oh, I know that if "it" happens, I might not face it as I now desire, but at least I want to remind myself of my idealistic intentions.

At a certain point there will be absolutely nothing I can do, but that is not the case now, nor in the immediate time ahead. Now I can do what strengthens and utilizes the mind—read and write and explore new things. But even more significantly, I want to live a spiritual life of surrender.

I live in the balancing act of doing that which I can, and, on the other hand, surrendering my entire life into God's hands, hands that so faithfully hold my life, including my mind, my intellect, my memory. Now I live by using my mind and if it is the final gift to give my Master, so be it. It is so important to give God my mind. I give it to God without argument or anger, but with absolute trust that God is bigger than anything that I can remember or logically comprehend.

The Apostle Paul wrote in Romans 12:1, "I appeal to you therefore, brothers and sisters, by the mercies of God, to present your bodies as a living sacrifice, holy and acceptable to God, which is your spiritual worship." At this moment I give God my mind and I want to remember to continue to give Him my intellect and memory until the end.

So, Stan, read and remember to live and age, and even die gracefully by surrendering all, even your mind, to the One who will always remember you.

Yours,

PS We live in the paradox between "making things happen" and "letting things happen." Much of our young life is lived in the realm of activity and accomplishment. I remember someone said, many decades ago, that sometimes when a door closes it means that God wants us to break the door down. That is the "be active and accomplish" side of life, but there are those, such as my wife, Diane, who live with the motto of "let things happen." This more passive stance of life is not passive at all. Rather the activities are those of waiting and surrendering.

The story of father Abraham hog-tying son Isaac and being willing to slit his throat is not comfortable bedtime reading for young children. Yet the call to surrender or to relinquish is the grindstone of sharpening that occurs for all faith-filled people. There are many ways to understand this story of Abraham and Isaac, but all of us at times are called to surrender those we love and that which we love. We are called to surrender our "make things happen" attitude of life and accept a "let things happen" attitude.

Jesus, in the Garden of Gethsemane, did not want to face the cross, but he was willing to say, "Yes," to his Abba Father. Everything from that moment on happened to Jesus, and God used what happened "to Jesus" for our benefit. It begins with surrender, a big "YES" to our Abba God.

How is it possible for us to surrender our lives, our minds, our loved ones, all to God? Henri Nouwen, in writing about the "Yes" of Jesus in the Garden, said:

> He (Jesus) possessed a trust beyond betrayal, a surrender beyond despair, a love beyond all fears. This intimacy beyond all human intimacies made it possible for Jesus to allow the request to let the cup pass him by to become a prayer directed to the one who had called him "My Beloved."
>
> Notwithstanding his anguish, that bond of love had not been broken. It couldn't be felt in the body, nor thought through in the mind. But it was there, beyond all feelings and thoughts, and it maintained the communion underneath all disruptions.
>
> It was that spiritual sinew, that intimate communion with his Father, that made him hold on to the cup and pray: "My Father, let it be as you, not I, would have it" (Matthew 26:39).
>
> (*Can You Drink the Cup,* Henri J.M. Nouwen, p. 41)

We are able to surrender for we know and have experienced the tremendous love of our Abba Father for us. His love for us sees "the big picture" of life and in that we trust, we wait, we surrender.

5

"JOURNEY"

October 20, 2010

Dear Stan,

As I write this letter, Diane and I are on a vacation journey to Whitefish, Montana. I call it a *journey* because the word *journey* is a concept that I always want to remember. All of life has been a journey and, therefore, it is full of surprises. There is always something new around the next bend, over the next hill, or around the corner. In this adventure of life, our God, who is the pioneer and perfecter of our faith (Hebrew 12:2) and of life itself, has not only gone before us in this journey, but is also a God of infinite surprise and adventure. As a God of surprise, God reveals Himself around each bend as newness, freshness, and adventure. There is no stagnation or boredom with God.

Since I am a pilgrim on a journey, I want to remember that this adventure of life also enters into the hallowed halls of older age and even the shadows of death. These are journeys that I have yet to take, but, perhaps, as I am reading these letters again, I might be on those paths. I want to have the mindset of the pilgrim for all of my life, whether on the paths of retirement or even the up-hill journey of illness or the quickly sloping (or slow meandering) paths to death. Even death is a new journey and I want to remember that as I enter that adventure, I do so with a trusted friend, Jesus. He has traversed that road before and, though it is all new for me, He knows the path well and will lead me "home."

Yes, I definitely want to remember life as an adventure, a journey, full of wonder and awe, full of pain and sorrow, and yet always full of surprise.

So, Stan, read and remember, live and age, and even die gracefully by remembering that all of life is a journey, full of surprises from the hand of our surprising God.

Yours,

PS People of faith know well the story of Sarah and Abraham and their journey of faith, but we often do not know the few verses preceding the faith journey. The writer of Genesis said:

> Terah took his son Abram and his grandson Lot son of Haran, and his daughter-in-law Sarai, his son Abram's wife, and they went out together from Ur of the Chaldeans to go into the land of Canaan; but when they came to Haran, they settled there. The days of Terah were two hundred five years; and Terah died in Haran. (Genesis 11: 31–32)

Terah started on a journey, a journey to the land of Canaan, but he stopped journeying, stopped moving forward. He settled down. Why? The narrative does not tell us, but we can speculate. Did he like the scenery? Was the journey too hard? We do not know why he settled down, but he did and the next verse is that he died in Haran. Settled down, stopped the journey, and then he died.

The narrative in Genesis continues:

> Now the LORD said to Abram, "Go from your country and your kindred and your father's house to the land that I will show you ..." So Abram went, as the LORD had told him; and Lot went with him. Abram was seventy-five years old when he departed from Haran. (Genesis 12:1–4)

Abram's life journey of faith was not a straight line, ever moving upward and onward in glory. He often got side-tracked, took things into his own hands and went in the wrong direction, but in the grand scheme of things, Abram, who became Abraham, journeyed forward in faith. Faith meant that Abram did not see the results or the reward of faith before him, but he journeyed by faith and not sight.

The Apostle Paul put it this way:

> So we do not lose heart. Even though our outer nature is wasting away, our inner nature is being renewed day by day. For this slight momentary affliction is preparing us for an eternal weight of glory beyond all measure, because we look not at what can be seen but at what cannot be seen; for what can be seen is temporary, but what cannot be seen is eternal. (2 Corinthians 4:16–18)

And the journey to what "cannot be seen" is especially true with our last breaths. We take those breaths, knowing that we are not alone and that the journey is just beginning.

6

"AGING AS OUR TEACHER"

October 21, 2010

Dear Stan,

The following are insights from my wife, Diane, and so by writing this I want to remember what I have learned from her. There are those who "fight" the aging process. "I'll beat this thing" expresses an impossibility, for we cannot "beat" old age or death. But we can embrace the journey. To embrace the journey is to welcome something rather than fight against it. To embrace old age is to welcome it as a friend, and even more as a teacher.

Diane's step-grandmother, Alice Hill, was a life-long learner, and Diane is a life-long learner in terms of being open to God's instruction or God's teaching in and through every phase of life. Aging is a process and in each step there is something new to learn.

The aging process can be our teacher if we embrace it as such. To fight getting older is to act as if one can control life and death, but that too is an illusion. Perhaps the opposite of trying to be in control is not passivity or total resignation, but rather an active attitude that welcomes everything as a teacher. God does not waste the "golden years" of our lives, but uses them for our transformation. So, Stan, what is it that God is teaching you at this point in your life? What is it you are to learn at this stage?

As I ponder those two questions I do not know what the lessons will be in the forthcoming years when I am reading this letter, but the questions are appropriate for the present as well as the future. Life seems to boil down to a simple word: *trust*! Whether it is in my present ministry situation of learning ministry in an entirely new type of setting for me here at Grace Lutheran or whether it was making the adjustments when our life journey drastically changed from living and working in Mexico to returning to the United States, the lesson is still *trust*. God is good and God knows what needs to take place in my life, and so I am called to trust.

So, Stan, read and remember, live and age, and even die gracefully by seeing all as a process of learning, a process of being "changed from one degree of glory to another" (2 Corinthians 3:18) for this is the work of the Spirit.

Yours,

PS   Kathleen Norris tells the story of a man who resisted change, resisted learning anything new. While in a tavern one day he heard some news concerning a schoolteacher whose student he had been decades before. "That old cow," he said. "She used to make me read. She said that I couldn't graduate till I read all she wanted. Well, I showed her; I haven't read a book since" (*Dakota: A Spiritual Geography,* p. 51). Learning, lifetime learning, comes from many sources including books, but each step of life is the opportunity to learn. To learn is to grow, to grow is to change.

The Harvard University longitudinal Study of Adult Development showed that lifetime learning is one of the key factors in aging well rather than aging in an unhealthy manner (George E. Vaillant, *Aging Well,* p. 213). Learning, obviously, expands one's scope of life, but it also gives a person motivation and vitality. Learning, putting it simply, makes life interesting.

7

"AGING AS OUR TEACHER: PART 2"

October 22, 2010

Dear Stan,

In this journey of life I am constantly changing, for I am constantly learning. Learning is change. There is the saying, "You can't teach an old dog new tricks," and carrying this forward we often think that as we age we cannot change, for we cannot learn new things. In the insightful book by Daniel J. Siegel called *Brainstorm* the author writes, "And when the brain gets activated, it can change the connections among neurons in a helpful way. Focusing the mind can change the structure of the brain *no matter our age* (italics mine)" (p. 50). So I want to keep learning.

In a book about aging Joan Chittister wrote:

> *A burden of these years is the fear that they bring*
> *nothing but incompetence to our once-competent selves.*
>
> *A blessing of these years is that we find ourselves at*
> *a time of life when we can finally concentrate on all*

the things we have ever wanted to learn and know and, as a result, become an even more important, more focused, more spiritual person than we have ever really been before. (The Gift of Years, p. 99)
Italics in the quote.

Being a lifetime learner is one thing. In this light I welcome new ideas, new thoughts. It was Bernard of Clairvaux (d. 1153) who said, "He who makes himself his own teacher becomes the pupil of a fool." I have often thought that I have very few, if any, original, creative ideas. Rather, most of my "creative ideas" are adaptions, developments of the thoughts of others. I build upon ideas of others and thereby continue to grow and learn.

But there is another side to this coin of learning: allowing our aging process itself to be our teacher. In this light I become attuned to what is taking place within me, around me, through me. I become aware of my pain and my joy, my inner thoughts and my feelings. I become aware of my body, my breath, my movement. I become aware and mindful of Immanuel, God in us, and the indwelling Spirit of God who is my teacher, my guide, and my inner light.

When I live life as if life is nothing but the outer world of activities, then I miss the richness of my interior life. There is more to life than activities. There is more to life than the situations that create pain or joy in my life. My reactions to life situations are important learning tools. How I feel, my inner thoughts are all important. Even an awareness of our bodies and our surroundings can be part of this inner journey of life.

Theologically we speak of *incarnation*, the eternal, the other, the holy God taking on flesh and blood in the person of Jesus the Christ, but incarnation continues as God comes to live within us. God's Spirit shows up in the "stuff of life," our bodies and our minds, our feelings and our intentions, our experiences and our reactions to those experiences. There is nothing outside of the scope of God, and the aging process itself can be and often is one of the teaching tools of the Spirit. I want to be open, receptive to all that God has to teach me.

So, Stan, read and remember, live and age, and even die gracefully by learning.

Yours,

8

"POSITIVE ATTITUDE/BE GRATEFUL"

October 23, 2010

Dear Stan,

My friend Terry Abell of Whitefish, Montana, who has ministered to many senior citizens through the years, wants to remember to always be positive and grateful.

There is a tremendous difference between being positive and grateful and working hard at being a positive thinker. There are many people who, by their sheer willpower or by natural disposition, have a positive outlook on life, and I am thankful for such people. Yet, Terry is thinking of something different, something deeper than a positive outlook on life. For Terry and myself, a positive attitude is a by-product of praise and gratitude toward God. When one sees life as a gift from God and as one knows of his or her eternal destination by grace through faith, praise and thanksgiving are the result and a positive attitude is a by-product. When God has captured our heart, then our perspective of life, our attitude toward life is transformed.

The Apostle Paul wrote, "Finally, beloved, whatever is true, whatever is honorable, whatever is just, whatever is pure, whatever is pleasing, whatever is commendable, if there is any excellence and if there is anything worthy of praise, think about these things" (Philippians 4:8). Such a mindset is possible because God is good and God desires good for His children, even though the pathway might be steep and treacherous. What a difference there is between a person who sees life from the perspective of the goodness of God and one who sees only the immediate difficulties and pains of aging.

It is fun to be around a person who is positive and who is grateful for the gift of life itself. Such attitudes are contagious, and I want to remember what God has done, what God has given so that I see life through God-given glasses, not simply "rose-tinted" glasses.

So, Stan, read and remember, live and age, and even die gracefully by looking to God's goodness and giving thanks and praise for who God is, what He has done and is doing, and for a future life face-to-face with Him.

Yours,

PS   Isn't it interesting how a number of people can see the same event, but report it in totally different ways, seeing the same event through totally different eyes?

The sixth century monk Dorotheos of Gaza told the story of three men passing another man on the street. One of the three looked at that fourth man and thought he was looking for a prostitute. Another of the three conjectured that the man was a thief, while the last individual imagined that he was on the way to meet a friend to pray.

All three men saw the same man, but each of them "saw" someone different, depending upon his own frame of reference. Patrick Henry wrote, "Sometimes people just don't see what they don't expect to find" (*The Ironic Christian's Companion*, p. 156). When our life is focused on God, then we begin to see God in everything and in so doing we live a life of gratitude.

Barbara Brown Taylor wrote, "Earth is so thick with divine possibility that it is a wonder we can walk anywhere without cracking our shins on altars" (*An Altar in the World,* p. 15). With this life-orientation, happiness is not found in simply having everything go "our way." Happiness is not getting what we want. Happiness flows from a life orientation that sees God, living and active, merciful and compassionate, present in all things and in all circumstances. Thus, we live lives of gratitude.

9

"LIFE DOESN'T CENTER IN PILLS"

October 28, 2010

Dear Stan,

"Let your speech always be gracious, seasoned with salt …" (Colossians 4:6). I have no idea what that means ("to be seasoned with salt") but I do know that it is really hard to be around the elderly who have only one topic of conversation: their aches and pains and illness. When life becomes so narrow that it can be measured in the size of a medicine pill, it is far too narrow.

I want to remember that life doesn't center in me, and especially not in my medicine cabinet. I want to remember to take an active interest in every person who comes into my field of vision, to ask him or her questions and to really listen to the answers. I want to be quick to hear and slow to speak (James 1:19), and when I speak I want my words to be those of the wise—a wisdom gained by continual learning. Lord, help me to grow in wisdom and not only in gray hair and flabby muscles.

I want to continue to take an interest in the world and its multi-colored events so that my talk can be relevant and I can continue to learn as well as have something to say. Lord, help me to be an interesting and relevant person, not one whose mind became solidified decades ago.

So, Stan, read and remember, live and age, and even die gracefully by listening intently, questioning respectfully, and sharing wisely.

Yours,

PS   This letter has been a concern for me. One of those who critiqued my early drafts asked, "What if life is down to pain and pills?" My pastoral walk with the ill and the dying has taken me alongside of those for whom life is "down to pain and pills." It seems as if there is nothing else in life but these two arduous enemies. And yet … is there not more? Is there not something, Someone bigger than pain and pills? Letter 17 speaks of one who has experienced the utter darkness and found God, but in this letter I want to remind myself of that which I can do, when I can do it. That is, I want to look beyond myself and my life situation to see others and thereby see God.

The Psalmist talked about how God had turned "my mourning into dancing" (Psalm 30:11). As long as the focus of our lives is on ourselves and on our situation, even our pain and our dying, our mourning cannot be turned into dancing. In the darkest periods of my life I realize that the focus of my life is myself. The more I can see only myself, the darker life becomes and the more life revolves around darkness, pills, and dying.

I have seen a loved one, a few days before her death, when death and dying might reasonably have been her primary focus, reach out with every ounce of strength she possessed and make the mark of the cross on the forehead of a young girl she had mentored during the healthier days of her life. Life was more than pills, it was more than dying. It was the giving of a blessing.

10

"PREMATURE DEATH"

November 2, 2010

Dear Stan,

My friend Carol shares her home with her mother, who is in her early nineties. Her mother is forever saying, "I just want to die. I have no reason to live. I have no reason to live." Carol wants to shout, "I'm your daughter! Aren't I enough to live for?"

Over and over again I have heard those who have prematurely died (that is, given up on life before their physical death) saying that they have no reason to live. I wonder what that means. Does it simply mean they can no longer do that which they have done before and, therefore, have no future, no hope, or no adventure left in their agenda of life?

Pastor and author Eugene Peterson wrote, "The terrible threat against life ... is not death, nor pain, nor any variation on the disasters that we so obsessively try to protect ourselves against with our social systems and personal strategies." Then he quotes Vitezslav Gardavsky, a Czech philosopher, "The terrible threat is that we might die earlier than we really do die, before death has become a natural necessity. The real horror lies in just such a premature death, a death after which we go on living for many years" (*Run with the Horses*, p. 21).

I do not want to die before my corporeal body takes its last breath. I do not want to be a walking (or sitting) cipher having no reason for taking up space and breathing valuable air. So as the years race by, I do not want my reason for living to get lost in the dust of more active, past years or even decades. Before I was born God called me, and gave me a reason for my existence as he did Jeremiah (Jeremiah 1:5).

And as I experience my less active years, God has not changed and still desires to use me in ways that are appropriate at this moment and this time in my life. God is the One who opens and closes doors. In the past I simply had to follow, and I have to do the same now. Those doors of opportunity and purpose will be proportional to my abilities at this age, but there will be something, someone right in front of me who needs me. Be alert.

So, Stan, read and remember, live and age, and even die gracefully by remembering that as long as you have breath, you have life.

Yours,

11

"DON'T POSTPONE LIVING"

November 3, 2010

Dear Stan,

I continue to ponder the theme of my previous letter, "Premature Death." I am reminded of the writing of Parker J. Palmer when he asserts that to be "fully alive is to act," and at the same time to be "fully alive is to contemplate" (*The Active Life*, p. 17). I might define *contemplation* a little differently than Palmer, but both action and reflection need to be aspects of a healthy life.

Erik Erikson in his classic theory on the eight stages of psychosocial development labels the stage from sixty-five to death as *Maturity*. He identifies the Basic Conflict of these years as Ego Identity vs. Despair and the important events of these years as Reflection on Life. This reflection on life is what I equate with Parker Palmer's *contemplation*. For Erik Erikson, reflection involved looking back on life and having a sense of fulfillment in our success or despair in our regrets.

For me, reflection allows me to look at what I am doing in the present, not simply the past, and how my relationships with people bring me a sense of life or a sense of death, even despair. When I am focused only upon myself, the end result is not life, but death. When my focus is upon others, upon the life experiences of those around me, then life is experienced, not death and despair.

In younger years the hectic pace and urgent demands of my life did not always allow for time to reflect. Now in the quieter years I have time, but reflection needs to be more than introspection. Reflection needs to be the openness, the availability, and the sensitivity to those around us.

"If only this ... if only that...." I have walked alongside people who live with regret. Regret can be the footprint of our lives as we look to the past. Or the past can be viewed as the "good old days," and there is a constant nostalgia for what has already been. For other people, the future is the time when they will "really live." They tend to postpone "living," thinking things will get better and then they can enjoy life.

Scripture says, "See, now is the acceptable time; see, now is the day of salvation" (2 Corinthians 6:2b). I do not think it is a stretch or Biblical heresy to also say, "Now is the day to live," and *Now* does not have age parameters on it. *Now* might have physical restrictions due to health limitations, but the Now of Life is always to be lived in God's abundance, not our limitations.

John O'Donohue wrote, "One of the greatest sins is the unlived life" (*Anam Cara*, p. 123). When we forever stand before a door and never open it, our lives become restricted, "unlived." In the second century the great Christian thinker Irenaeus said, "The glory of God is the human person fully alive." To be "fully alive" is not age dependent.

> *A burden of these years is the temptation to cling*
> *to the times and things behind us rather than*
> *move to the liberating moments ahead.*

*A blessing of these years is the invitation to go
lightfooted into the here and now—because we
spend far too much of life preparing for the
future rather than enjoying the present.*
(*The Gift of Years,* Joan Chittister, p. 93)

So, Stan, read and remember, live and age, and even die gracefully by living fully in the present.

Yours,

12

"CLUTTER"

March 18, 2011

Dear Stan,

How many families have you watched that have had to sort through a lifetime of hoarding that their loved ones had accumulated through the decades and all that "stuff" is now left to those who remain? Stan, remember that you do not want your loved ones to have to clean up your mess after you die because you were too lazy or too much a coward to take care of the details and the clutter of your life while you were able.

The attic is full. The closets have boxes of stuff. The memorabilia weigh in at tons and what are your children going to do with all of it? So, Stan, on those rainy days, use the time to go through your closets and your boxes and be willing to throw away, give away, or designate things to your family.

But a word to the wise—don't get rid of things that your family would want later on. Remember how your sons, Andrew and Peter, forever brought to your memory that you put their Nintendo up for sale without asking them? It is far better to ask for permission beforehand than have to ask for forgiveness afterward.

So, Stan, read and remember, live and age, and even die gracefully by taking responsibility for "messes" and accumulations so that your loved ones are not stuck with a "mess."

Yours,

PS   It takes time, energy, but above all willingness to begin to "size down." For some people who see this task as formidable as climbing Mt. Everest, it might mean that you hire a "professional" to help you sort through the "stuff." There seems to be a fundamental, spiritual attitude or issue at stake even before we begin this momentous spring cleaning. The question is: "Can we **let go** of things?"

We might even be aware of Jesus' admonition that life does not consist of the abundance of our possessions (Luke 12:15). But we might justify ourselves by straining our necks looking toward our neighbor who has so much more stuff in comparison to ourselves. Such comparisons do not help us to downsize, but rather motivate us to accumulate even more.

We might even be familiar with the New Testament story of the "Rich Young Ruler" who wanted to follow Jesus but was unwilling to "let go" of his millions, his large bank account, his closets and rooms of hoarding (Luke 18:18ff). Yet we hold on to our stuff so that our stuff becomes a burden to our loved ones.

The first disciples were told by their leader Jesus to "take nothing for your journey" (Luke 9:3). The modus operandi was to "travel light." The years have passed and the stuff, the clutter has piled high. Everything has become important, everything has special memories, everything, all of our stuff, begins to give us our identity. Instead of "traveling light" we find our identity, our personhood in the things we possess, or, rather, the things that possess us. Maybe it is time to "let go" and at least "travel lighter"!

13

"TAKE TIME TO LISTEN"

July 20, 2011

Dear Stan,

One of my favorite books is *Out of Solitude* by Henri J.M. Nouwen. It is, in my estimation, a classic in terms of understanding prayer and the Christian life. In addressing the need for true *care* for others he wrote, "Every human being has a great, yet often unknown, gift to care, to be compassionate, to become present to the other, to listen, to hear and to receive. If that gift would be set free and made available, miracles could take place" (p. 40).

I often ponder how is such "other-centeredness" ignited in a person? Again Nouwen urges us to follow the pattern of Jesus and withdraw, to spend time in quietness and solitude with our God. "Then your concern for others can be motivated more by their needs than your own. In short: then you can care. Let us therefore live our lives to the fullest but let us not forget to once in a while get up long before dawn to leave the house and go to a lonely place" (*ibid.*, p. 26).

A number of years ago in the announcement time during Sunday morning worship, I shared with my congregation that my wife, Diane, and I would be presenting a forty-hour workshop in which participants would learn how to listen to others who are going through painful and difficult times. I explained that as Christians we are called to love others and one of the primary ways that we can express that love is through listening.

As she left worship that day, Ruth, a member of the congregation, left a part of her understanding of life and faith with me. She shook my hand at the door and added these words, "You can't teach someone to love. They either have it, or they don't." Then she left. I did not get a chance at that time to listen to the rest of her story, but even those words shout a message of hurt and pain.

I need to take time with others, to listen and to really care for other people as persons, as individuals. I also need to take time with God for the Holy Spirit to work in my life and move me from self-absorption to love, but I can also learn, learn how to listen to others, for a listening ear is perhaps the strongest medicine needed for my soul.

So, Stan, read and remember, live and age, and even die gracefully by remembering to take time to care by listening, to listen to God and to listen to others.

Yours,

14

"SELF-ABSORPTION / FAN THE FLAMES OF LOVE"

July 29, 2011

Dear Stan,

Today is the last of eight days camping at Mary Hill State Park in the Columbia Gorge. As we arrived, the fires of love between Diane and me were at the stage of smoldering embers, embers that were growing dark with the shades of death. We had arrived at this wintry death through our own paths of self-absorption, and the inertia of stagnation seemed greater than the pull of desire to return to the spring of love. But we had given ourselves eight days to be together, to live simply, to share, to talk, to listen. Fuel was added to the fire. The dark clouds of a mournful winter began to roll away to the awakening dawn of spring and love was reborn, rekindled as the dying campfire once again came to dancing life.

Stan, what is there to remember from this experience of restoring, refreshing camping? At any stage of life, through all the meandering journeys of life, self-absorption can cause love to atrophy. It is said that there are certain types of cancer that, if detected early, have a 100% cure rate, but if not, will progress to death. Self-absorption is a cancer to the soul and to the health and vitality of relationships. If undetected, the result is death. Stan, remember that life is more than you!

The healing, restorative process took time—eight days of sharing and listening and being touched by the pain stories of the other. Remember that all your relationships take time and these need to be times of really hearing the inner pain stories of the other person. This cannot happen as you sit in front of the death-inducing TV or as you run to the next event on your busy calendar. It takes time to be with another—to really be present to another—especially those who are in your daily radar and who easily become overlooked because of familiarity.

So, Stan, read and remember, live and age, and even die gracefully by taking time with your loved ones, asking penetrating questions, listening with a caring heart, and sharing equally of your joys and sorrows.

Yours,

15

"STAY ACTIVE"

July 30, 2011

Dear Stan,

I saw an "old" couple today. Isn't it interesting how "old" is so very relative. This couple was perhaps ten or more years older than I am. They were at Mary Hill State Park where Diane and I have been camping.

They too were camping. No, they did not have a tent as we do, nor had they joined the "motor home throng." They simply had a van and they and their three dogs slept in the van.

So often I hear people complain that they cannot do this or they cannot do that. They complain that they do not have enough money to allow them to go out to fancy restaurants every week. Complaint about their limitations is the selected conversation topic of the day for many people, but this older couple that I saw today did not focus on what they could not do, but they did what they *could* do. Perhaps they were no longer able to sleep in a small tent on the hard ground or perhaps they could not afford a large, or even small, motor home, but those limitations did not keep them housebound, frozen in front of the brain-killer TV. Instead they used what they had, a van, and they continued their active life.

Stan, as you continue to stumble along in the aging process, do what you can instead of complaining about what you cannot do. You will have to make adjustments and even change activities, but stay active, do not quit living before you quit breathing.

Paul wrote about being content in Philippians 4:11b–13: "for I have learned to be content with whatever I have. I know what it is to have little, and I know what it is to have plenty. In any and all circumstances I have learned the secret of being well fed and of going hungry, of having plenty and of being in need. I can do all things through him who strengthens me." At whatever stage of life that you find yourself, receive it as a gift and do what you can, for God's presence is seen in what we have, not what we do not have.

So, Stan, read and remember, live and age, and even die gracefully by remembering to stay active—as active as you are able—instead of complaining about what you cannot do.

Yours,

16

"SIGNS OF HOPE"

July 31, 2011

Dear Stan,

The "older couple" camping in a van at Mary Hill State Park continues to ignite ideas within my mind. I realize that it is the little things that I do and that others do that are "signs of hope." Even as I watched this couple at Mary Hill State Park, their action of camping in a van gave hope for my tomorrow.

E.B. White (1899–1985) was a prolific and influential writer and essayist. In *Letters of Note* compiled by Shaun Usher there is a letter from White to a Mr. Nadeau. Apparently Mr. Nadeau, as so many other people, had become overwhelmed by "the state of affairs" of humankind. Nadeau sought E.B. White's wisdom and insight into the future of the human race.

E.B. White responded in 1973 with a well-crafted letter, now titled *Wind the Clock*. In part it reads:

> As long as there is one upright man, as long as there is one compassionate woman, the contagion may spread and the scene is not desolate. Hope is the thing that is left to us, in a bad time. I shall get up Sunday morning

and wind the clock, as a contribution to order and steadfastness. ... Hang on to your hat. Hang on to your hope. And wind the clock, for tomorrow is another day. (*Letters of Note,* compiled by Shaun Usher, p. 10)

Some people look at the world's situation with pessimism and defeatism. Their whole psyche is riddled with a "do nothing" attitude, for they see all as hopeless. E.B. White's answer to that is "wind the clock," do what is in front of you, no matter how little, how seemingly inconsequential.

The year was 587 B.C. and the prophet Jeremiah's predictions of the destruction of Jerusalem were about to be realized. With the army of Nebuchadnezzar pounding on the gates of Jerusalem, and the people within the walled city dying of starvation, panic, and hopelessness, Jeremiah wound the clock. That is, as a sign of hope, hope for God's future, Jeremiah bought a field. The price must have been dirt cheap, and as Eugene Peterson wrote, "He didn't buy the field on the advice of his broker, but by the leading of God" (*Run with the Horses*, p. 175). Property values must have plummeted to basement levels, but Jeremiah, from behind prison walls, confined for prophesying concerning the fall of Jerusalem, responded with a simple, life-oriented action of buying a field.

Perhaps, as darkness clouds my eyesight, and my limbs become more arthritic, I need to find simple acts of faith and hope, acts that tell myself and the world that there is still hope.

Eugene Peterson quoted G.K. Chesterton on the subject of hope: "As long as matters are really hopeful, hope is mere flattery or platitude. It is only when everything is hopeless that hope begins to be a strength at all. Like all the Christian virtues, it is as unreasonable as it is indispensable" (*ibid.*, p. 172).

So, Stan, read and remember, live and age, and even die gracefully by remembering to find hope for living, and remember to be a sign of hope for others that they too might have a reason for living.

Yours,

17

"FINAL BLESSINGS"

November 14, 2011

Dear Stan,

I always want to remember Cal Johnson. At this point in my life he has taught me more about "dying well" than any other person. Yes, remember Cal and the blessing that he gave his family and others as he faced his death. He knew he would die from pancreatic cancer, but how would he die? How would he face his death? He did it with such grace that it is etched in my mind forever.

I have watched so many people face their death. Some do it very badly, others thoughtlessly, but not Cal. Cal was a quiet, stoic Swede who lived most of his life in the public eye as the principal of a local high school, but he maintained his private, non-emotional outlook on life. He faced his journey with cancer in the manner of Jacob in the Old Testament: with great dignity, open honesty, true grace, and even with very appropriate emotion.

It was Palm Sunday, Passion Sunday, and Cal and his family circled around the altar in his home church of Immanuel Lutheran near Everson, Washington. Bread and wine were to be served, the body and blood of Cal's Lord and

Savior were to be shared. After the service Cal slowly, deliberately proceeded to each member of his large, extended family. To each person he gave a hug and an expression of thanks for his or her presence with him during this time of impending death, which he faced with a hope for an eternal future.

Instead of fighting the inevitable, Cal used this time to visit with family and friends who came from far and near to see him. He was pure gift to each person and each one was, in turn, a gift to him. Cal demonstrated in his dying process an openness and a transparency about his condition, but he also demonstrated his ongoing interest in, concern for, and willingness to give to others.

So, Stan, read and remember, live and age, and even die gracefully by remembering to be a blessing to others and be willing to proclaim a blessing to others, thereby allowing your dying processes to be the last gift that you give to those you love and who love you.

Yours,

PS   I have seen such a blessing given even more recently, and this time from a loved one, one who was the closest to me. She had lain in her hospice bed for a number of days without talking, with limited response to the many people who had come to see her, and then it happened.

A young woman whom she had mentored came to say her "good-byes," and again there was limited response, but as the young woman was about to leave, my beloved used every ounce of energy she possessed, with one hand lifting up the other, she made the mark of the cross on this young woman's forehead. A blessing! A blessing to be remembered by this young woman and by me for as long as we live.

We all die, but do we do so by giving blessings to those we love?

18

"GIVE CHOCOLATE"

March 23, 2012

Dear Stan,

And now there are George and Joan to remember, and from whom life-improving lessons can be learned. During the nearly fourteen years that I knew Joan, she was often sick. She spent many, many months in the University of Washington Medical Center, among numerous other hospitals and nursing homes. Through all that "hospital experience" Joan could have accumulated a long list of nurses and medical aids who cared for her with grumpy attitudes and less than compassionate or even skillful hands, but she did not.

Joan did, with the help of her husband, George, what I have seen no one else do. On the tray beside her bed, Joan had a large bowl full of bite-sized chocolate bars. They were not for her, but for those who cared for her and those who came to visit her. "Thank you" was being expressed by Joan and by George in words and in chocolate! What a delicious way of expressing gratitude!

Stan, remember that caregivers, nurses, nurses' aides, and all those who serve you need to be appreciated, and a word of thanks, as well as a bite of chocolate, can sustain and encourage their hearts. As a result Joan consistently received excellent care, for her attitudes and actions elicited the best from her caregivers. Maybe the Scripture adage is correct: "You reap what you sow." Sow chocolate and, Stan, you will reap care and compassion.

So, Stan, read and remember, live and age, and even die gracefully by remembering to say, "Thank you," and give away chocolate!

Yours,

PS   There are those who have a hard time saying, "Thank you," let alone demonstrating thankfulness in tangible ways. The Scriptures are full of admonitions about being thankful to God for God's continued gifts given to us, but I cannot bring to mind anything in Scripture about our need to be thankful to each other. Of course, we are to "love our neighbor as ourselves" (Mark 12:31). And definitely thanking others is a sign of loving others.

There are so many ways we love others. There are tangible gifts that we give. Two ears and a receptive heart are truly gifts of love given to others. We love others as we offer forgiveness for the pains that are inflicted, either knowingly or unknowingly, upon us. But when our lives are carrying heavy burdens, and the skies are gray with ominous storms and we can still think of others by giving chocolates as tangible acts of love, then we are truly loving our neighbor as ourselves.

John O'Donohue speaks of the blessing of others through our generosity: "A generous heart is never lonesome. A generous heart has luck. The lonesomeness of contemporary life is partly due to the failure of generosity (*Eternal Echoes,* p. 216).

19

"MOUNTAINS CLIMBED FROM A WHEELCHAIR"

June 15, 2012

Dear Stan,

What a weekend! Maybe the lessons learned can continue to have significance for me and for others for a long time to come. After driving across the state of Washington to deliver Andrew at a friend's home in the Palouse Country of southeast Washington, Diane and I drove up to Spokane to visit Bob and Pat Moylan.

Bob is now in his late seventies. He has been a mentor and friend to me for many years. I asked Bob, "What would you want to remind yourself of in the years to come?"

His answer was firm and certain: "There are no problems that cannot be overcome." Is this memory note simply "possibility thinking"? Is it an unrealistic image of life? No, it is so much more for Bob. He knows, he daily experiences the reality of that statement.

Many people say, "Growing old isn't for cowards," for they know the immense mountains that have to be scaled in the cycle of life when mountain climbing is all but impossible. Shortly after Bob's retirement from Trinity Lutheran College, where he was the Academic Dean and known as Dr. Robert Moylan, he began an arduous mountain climb of muscular dystrophy. As the years have progressed and his body has steadily deteriorated, Bob has learned that he has a rare form of the disease. There are only about five hundred such cases worldwide.

For Bob and his faithful wife, Pat, the aging journey has been a gargantuan mountain climb. His latest development is that he is no longer able to be in the swimming pool or to walk at all. Yet, in facing that sheer granite precipice, Bob wants to remember always that there are no problems that cannot be overcome.

What does that mean? It does not mean that the Mt. Everest of M.D. will be removed and he will walk on a level plain again. No, Bob will probably die from complications from M.D. Each and every challenge will be faced—honestly, prayerfully, and with all the creative thinking that is possible. Bob's God Almighty, Bob's faithful God will continue to lead and guide him, his wife, and those who care for him.

The challenges in front of him will not crush him, for he is more than the problem and his God is more than a God who deals with problems. God is a God of LIFE!

So, Stan, read and remember, live and age, and even die gracefully by remembering Bob Moylan and the "mountains" he climbed in his wheelchair, and yet he faced those mountains by living, praying, thinking, and overcoming.

Yours,

PS "Mountains" come in many sizes and shapes, just as do our problems. Think with me of the mountains faced by the women and men of Scripture.

- The Canaanite woman faced a gender barrier and an ethnic barrier but she continued steadfast in her persistent petition of Jesus concerning the need for healing for her daughter (Matthew 15:21–28).
- Moses faced the water barrier on one side and the pursuing Egyptian army on the other side (Exodus 14:1–14).
- The Apostle Paul's juggernaut of opposition included violent opposition, shipwrecks, misunderstandings, and much, much more (2 Corinthians 6:4–10).
- Zacchaeus had such a size differential that he needed a handy tree (Luke 19:1–10).

The "mountains" are legion and at times even faith cannot seem to move them. Paul was given a "thorn in the flesh," which constantly jabbed him (2 Corinthians 12:7–10). Even his faithful prayers could not move this thorny mountain, but he learned that some thorns and some mountains are present in our lives, not to enlarge our calf muscles, but to enhance our vision to see the invisible. Paul was to learn that God's grace and grace alone was enough. He did not have to "overcome" his thorny mountain, rather he rested in the sufficiency of God's grace.

I think of Joni Eareckson Tada who was paralyzed in a diving accident when she was very young. In the years following the accident she went to faith healers, but nothing happened … or did it? No, she was not healed so that she could throw away her wheelchair, but through time Joni began to "overcome" her mountain of being a quadriplegic by means of God's sufficient grace, a grace that has empowered her to live and to serve and to rejoice as one who is paralyzed. God did not pass her by, God did not abandon her, but God did begin to transform the way she prayed and, consequently, the way she lived.

Yes, Joni and Bob are swimming in the same sea, the sea of God's sufficient grace, God's overcoming grace.

20

"MEMORIES"

October 5, 2012

Dear Stan,

Last night I sat around the dining room table of my older brother Albin and his wife, Alice. We reminisced about growing up, remembering some of the stories and events that shaped our lives. My brother and I have two different approaches to life and to remembering the past. There is not a right and wrong in our approaches, but rather we have each chosen a unique way to help us deal with the pain stories of the past.

One way, my brother's chosen method and the method of many people, is to choose to remember, talk about, and focus upon those memories that are positive, joyful, and uplifting. With this method one remembers the good things and, consequently, one does not become depressed or sad over past events that were painful and difficult.

I have chosen to remember the past in a different way. I am who I am today and will be in the future because of both the painful events and the joy-filled events of the past. I do not want to be afraid of remembering both. I do not want to dwell on the negative, but I do want to embrace them, accept them, and thank God for even those events, for I have been shaped and molded through the Potter's hands that have at times been hard to experience.

To embrace the pain stories means to me to remember them and share them when appropriate. It is not to "villainize" others, but to accept them all as tools of the Master. It is to see in the pain God's grace that has sustained me, taught me, and molded me. It is to see how God is bigger than the pain stories and how God has continued to be faithful in all events.

So, Stan, read and remember, live and age, and even die gracefully by remembering all of life, the good and the bad and the ugly, as events that God has used to shape who you are.

Yours,

PS My understanding of life has been shaped by the writings of Henri Nouwen and the emphasis of this letter in remembering the painful as well as the joyful events of life can be seen in Nouwen's following writing:

"If God is found in our hard times, then all of life, no matter how apparently insignificant or difficult, can open us to God's work among us. ... We tend, however, to divide our past into good things to remember with gratitude and painful things to accept or forget. This way of thinking, which at first glance seems quite natural, prevents us from allowing our whole past to be the source from which we live our future. It locks us into a self-involved focus on our gain or comfort. It becomes a way to categorize and, in a way, control. Such an outlook becomes another attempt to avoid facing our suffering. Once we accept this division, we develop a mentality in which we hope to collect more good memories than bad memories, more things to be glad about than things to be resentful about, more things to celebrate than to complain about." (*The Dance of Life,* pp. 164–165)

21

"UTTER DARKNESS"

October 15, 2012

Dear Stan,

How important are these letters to me? The longer it takes for me to compile these letters, the more I realize I am forgetting the little details of life from the past and even the present. Those details include some of the learnings, the insights that are coming my way, things that might be important to remember as my aging mind continues to naturally melt away, as a snowman melts on a warm winter's day.

Last night I had a long phone conversation with dear friends Gary and Martha. Martha suffers from the pernicious enemy of mind, body, and emotions: Parkinson's disease. She was trying to describe the horrendous, stifling attacks of anxiety that beset her. She quoted another friend who suffers from another debilitating, fatal disease: "At times all I can do is go into the utter darkness and there is God."

I have not experienced "utter darkness" in the light of day or even in the darkness of night. My life thus far is at times lived in the brilliance of the sun, in the gloom of the shadows, or even in the confusion of the fog, but utter darkness—no, that has not been part of my life thus far. But perhaps it too will be part of my journey in the future. Perhaps my days will no longer be experienced from the brilliance of the sun, but rather from the fearfulness of "utter darkness." Yes, from this vantage point of life, "utter darkness" seems extremely horrifying, utterly, utterly terrifying, but if that is to be my experience, Stan, remember this conversation:

"There I find God."

So, Stan, read and remember, live and age, and even die gracefully by remembering that in the "utter darkness" of life you will not be alone, but there you will, once again, find your Friend.

Yours,

PS   St. John of the Cross (1542–1591) consistently used the phrase "the dark night of the soul." He would resonate with Martha's friend who in utter darkness found God. St. John shares his mysticism, his sensual understanding of God's coming to him in the utter darkness of life in the following poem:

The Dark Night

> One dark night
> Fired with love's urgent longings
> —Ah, the sheer grace!—
> I went out unseen,
> My house being now all stilled.
>
> In darkness, and secure,
> By the secret ladder, disguised,

—Ah, the sheer grace!—
In darkness and concealment,
My house being now all stilled;

On that glad night,
In secret, for no one saw me,
Nor did I look at anything,
With no other light or guide
Than the one that burned in my heart;

This guided me
More surely than the light of noon
To where He waited for me
Him I knew so well—
In a place where no one else appeared.

O guiding night!
O night more lovely than the dawn!
O night that has united
The Lover with His beloved,
Transforming the beloved in her Lover.

Upon my flowering breast
Which I kept wholly for Him alone,
There He lay sleeping,
And I caressing Him
There in the breeze from the fanning cedars.

When the breeze blew from the turret
Parting His hair,
He wounded my neck
With His gentle hand,
Suspending all my senses.

STAN JACOBSON

I abandoned and forgot myself,
Laying my face on my Beloved;
All things ceased; I went out from myself,
Leaving my cares
Forgotten among the lilies.
(from *John of the Cross for Today: The Ascent,* Susan Muto, pp. 14–15)

22

"WHEN?"

October 28, 2012

Dear Stan,

How will I know when the time has come for me to stop driving a car? How will I know when to move from our private home into some type of assisted care unit? It is said that "timing is everything," and I am sure that is true concerning many issues in life. In my pastoral ministry I have known so many families that have struggled with their elderly parents' refusal to stop driving or their refusal to move out of their homes, even though they are no longer safe while driving or in living alone.

The question of "When?" was answered for me lately as I talked with David Head, a member of Grace Lutheran Church, the congregation I pastor. He described how he had signed a contract with his adult children giving them veto power. I asked, "Veto power over what?" He explained that later in his life, when he might be unaware of the danger he is causing by still driving, his children will have veto power over his decision to remain behind the wheel. He will trust his children's ultimate decision rather than his own at a time when his decision-making process might be too strongly influenced by the fear of losing his independence, or simply the inability to effectively self-reflect or evaluate his own actions.

That is a wise decision! Such a decision demands a great deal of humility, a great deal of open communication, and unbelievable trust—trust not only in God but in the judgment of one's children. To me such a decision is a demonstration of one who is truly wise.

So, Stan, read and remember, live and age, and even die gracefully by remembering to be wise in your decision-making processes.

Yours,

PS   There is an interesting story in the book of 2 Samuel where King David offers the aged Barzillai the opportunity to come to Jerusalem and live out his days in the care of the King. Barzillai answers King David, "How many years have I still to live, that I should go up with the king to Jerusalem? Today I am eighty years old; can I discern what is pleasant and what is not? Can your servant taste what he eats or what he drinks? Can I still listen to the voice of singing men and singing women? Why then should your servant be an added burden to my lord the king? Please let your servant return, so that I may die in my own town, near the graves of my father and my mother. But here is your servant Chimham; let him go over with my lord the king; and do for him whatever seems good to you" (2 Samuel 19:34–35, 37). Barzillai faces his life realistically and forthrightly. At the same time he seeks to look out for the welfare of his son.

23

"WISDOM OF THE AGED"

November 5, 2012

Dear Stan,

"The wisdom of the aged!" One would hope that as a person grows older, he or she also grows wiser. As a young man, Solomon asked for wisdom, but as he grew older it seems as if his wisdom fled as fast as his years advanced. I hope that will not be my case.

As I ponder wisdom now, in the quietness of my early morning devotional time, something has come to my mind that I want to remember in the years ahead. Often I have heard adults pontificate to those younger, "This is how I did it when I was your age." People want to share their past experiences as if their experiences have universal truth and can be applied by all, in all circumstances and for all generations. This seems very doubtful to me.

I wonder if people use their past experiences and even their inner thoughts, as I am in these letters, to validate their existence, their experience, their "wisdom." Perhaps we tell our stories around a cup of coffee in order not only to "be known," but to somehow say to the world or even to ourselves, *I exist and what I experienced still has importance.*

But let me get back to wisdom. I want to remember that wisdom is not telling people how I did things in the past, but rather listening to others and, in listening, helping them to draw out of themselves their own wisdom. When I have the urge to simply talk about myself, I know I am not acting wisely. Wisdom listens.

Another thought came to me this morning as I was reading Parker Palmer's *Let Your Life Speak*. Perhaps there is more universal wisdom found in our "mistakes" than in our "successes." I want to always remember that when the opportunity to share my past experiences arises, I do not want to share only the heart-warming, positive experiences, but I want to remember to share my failures and my struggles also. Perhaps there is a greater connection with others in the struggles and failures than in the times when all the pieces of the puzzle fit together.

So, Stan, read and remember, live and age, and even die gracefully by remembering to be "wise," wise in how you listen, wise in what you share, and be willing to reveal the challenges as well as the struggles.

Yours,

PS   Dietrich Bonhoeffer gave us some very pointed words on our need to listen to each other:

> "The first service that one owes to others in the fellowship consists in listening to them. Just as love to God begins with listening to His Word, so the beginning of love for the brethren is learning to listen to them. ... Christians, especially ministers, so often think they must always contribute something when they are in the company of others, that this is the one service they have to render. They forget that

listening can be a greater service than speaking. ... He who can no longer listen to his brother will soon no longer be listening to God either; he will be doing nothing but prattle in the presence of God too. ... Anyone who thinks that his time is too valuable to spend keeping quiet will eventually have no time for God and his brother, but only for himself and for his own follies" (*Life Together*, p. 97f).

24

"FAMILY HISTORY"

December 7, 2012

Dear Stan,

It seems as if it is a black hole or an insurmountable wall. Cousin Elaine has done remarkable research into the family history on my mother's side, and this information takes us back into the 1400s in our native land of Finland. Then there is my dad's side of the family where the information ends with my grandparents, a seeming void, black hole, or an informationless wall. No one even knows the stories of how my own parents met or what their early lives were like. Now all have passed through the veil of death, taking their stories with them.

How I now would like to know more about my parents and grandparents and even beyond! Those unknown stories are part of my invisible genetic code and I want to understand. I want to know who I am in terms of the stories of my ancestral lineage. I am a melding of stories and the creation of new stories. Even much of the Bible was originally the product of the storytellers' memory.

But this yearning to know story has not always been present in me, and was not the motivating force propelling me to ask questions and listen to the answers of my parents. For the past four decades it has been too late to ask and to listen.

So now I want to remind myself to tell the stories of my known life, to let my sons know the stories of their parents and grandparents. Perhaps they are not ready for their yearning spirits to gather such a treasure chest of history, but I want to find ways to preserve the stories until the time of their second or third birth, their longing to know their history that reaches beyond the moment. Yes, I want to remember to write, to record the narrative.

So, Stan, read and remember, live and age, and even die gracefully by remembering to tell and record your history, your story so that in years to come the future generations will have some answers to the longings of their hearts.

Yours,

PS   As I write this postscript I have recently returned from a six-day road trip with my elder brother Albin. He is approaching eighty-one years of age. This road trip was an opportunity for him to see parts of Washington State that he has never seen, and it was an opportunity for me to spend valuable time with him, asking questions that drew out stories from his life journey and from parts of mine also.

Joan Chittister wrote that memory "is a wild horse, unbridled, riderless, maverick" (*The Gift of Years*, p. 153). Memory lived in one's mind is grounding and even cathartic, but memory shared with eager listeners is life-unifying and opens all to the possibilities of life.

25

"FACING DEATH"

July 12, 2014

Dear Stan,

After a long hiatus of over a year and a half I am once again writing to myself, but as I write this letter our lives are on a "shutdown mode." That isn't exactly right, for we—our entire family—are living each moment the best we can in a state of alertness as we look death in the eye!

Maybe I am writing this not so much to remember insights, insights that might be important later in my life, but rather as a means of my own cathartic healing, for Diane is dying. It is not easy to write, but perhaps I need it. I don't know what I need right now. All I know is that I am sitting down to write after a long absence and the pain of Diane's forthcoming death is very, very real.

Diane is dying. There is no comfortable, uplifting way to say it. She is dying and we are on a twenty-four-hour watch with her to see when this dreaded enemy slithers into the fragile body of my beloved wife.

So much has happened since I last wrote so that there is a need for a historical, emotional, personal catch-up of events. There really are two stories here, the one immediately facing me every second of the day and night, and the other involving the events leading up to the death of Diane's mother, Hazelle, on June 17, 2013. In this letter, because everything is so fresh, so real, so imminent, I will begin with Diane's story and then in another letter remind myself about Hazelle.

Diane's story began many years ago, perhaps two, three, four—who knows? It began in silence and continued in silence. It began as an unnoticeable, unwanted, invading presence, a cancer cell. No one knows when, no one knows how, no one knows why, but that non-small cell lung cancer began its merciless invasion in Diane's right lung.

It was in February 2013, while vacationing in New Zealand and visiting friends there, that I first noticed something was wrong. Diane did not have the stamina, the energy of the Diane that I knew. I was concerned that it might be her heart, but talking about health issues was not something Diane ever wanted to do. Sometime after returning home from New Zealand, Diane began to cough, only a slight cough at first and as the months progressed the cough increased. No amount of encouraging her to see a doctor accomplished anything, until at a Seattle Mariner baseball game, one of our son Andrew's friends looked at Diane and said, "You have to see a doctor," and the words struck home.

On June 21, 2013, Diane saw a doctor and discovered that she had a collapsed lung. Three days later she discovered that she had Stage IV non-small cell lung cancer. Those are the facts, but facts are only that: facts, history. That does not tell the shock, the horror. The radiologist said, "One year." The oncologist said, "Two years, possibly three," and now it is going on thirteen months since we heard that life-altering word *cancer*.

STAN JACOBSON

I will not document the journey of the past thirteen months. It is too much to write, too painful, and yet at the same time too amazing to describe. Perhaps at another time, in another document, but for now I needed to write just this.

So, Stan, read and remember, live and age, and even die gracefully by remembering this journey, this journey that changed your life.

Yours,

26

"THE END / THE BEGINNING, FOR BOTH OF US"

July 25, 2014

Dear Stan,

The watch is over. Death came knocking at the door on July 18, 2014, and Diane ever so quietly, ever so peacefully slipped out the back door holding the hand of Jesus. Son Andrew, son Peter and his wife, Paulie, an adopted family member and caregiver Barbara, our Associate Pastor Jason, and I were present. We watched, we prayed, we sat and stood in silence in the comfort of our home. Jason sang quietly the old hymns of faith, and we watched. Andrew suggested we sing "Danny Boy," in honor of Diane's Irish heritage and so they sang, but I watched. It was as if she quietly slipped out the back door, while no one was watching. She exited ever so quietly, ever so peacefully, ever so gracefully. And the end came.

Diane was not afraid. She was at peace, at rest. Though she had not communicated with us for a couple of days, she passed through the veil of death in peace.

STAN JACOBSON

Oh, we all know it is but the beginning for Diane, but it is also the end, the end of her journey on earth, her journey with me, at least literally, physically present. It is the end, and now I begin a new journey.

So, Stan, read and remember, live and age, and even die gracefully by remembering.

Yours,

27

"A PHYSICAL REMINDER"

July 27, 2014

Dear Stan,

This morning I put a Bible on a stand in a prominent place beside the TV. I do not know how long it will be there, but for now it has important lessons that I want to remember. The Bible is not to be a "room decoration," but rather a physical remembrance. Maybe it is similar to the pile of rocks, the memorial that Israel built after they traversed the Jordan River into the Promised Land. The pile of rocks was to be a memorial, a reminder of what God had done for them (Joshua 4:1–9).

First, every time I see the Bible on the stand, I want to remember that I am not alone. It feels as if I am. The house is silent. The boys have left, the phone has not rung. The house is silent, unless I have the TV on or music playing. Diane is no longer here. Her presence no longer fills the space with life, with warmth, with love. Yes, it feels as if I am alone.

But, the Bible, in a prominent place, reminds me that God is present. In the midst of loneliness and grief I need to be reminded. It is too easy for me to slide down the ravine of depression when I feel absolutely alone. I need to be reminded ALWAYS that I am not alone. God, Emmanuel—God with us, with me—is present and when God is present, God is active.

Secondly, I need to be reminded that God desires to speak to me. The Scriptures are the primary enfleshment of the Voice of God for me, but the Spirit speaks in a myriad of ways. So, Stan, LISTEN. When you are all alone, enter into the Living Voice of God. Do not designate or limit God to your "quiet time" in the morning. Listen always!

Stan, the enthroned Word is also there as a reminder for you to grieve well. As I write this it has been only nine days since your Beloved journeyed where you cannot go—yet. In the silence, in the aloneness, remember to grieve and remember that God cries with you. It is easy to push grief aside, to bury grief by burying yourself in the TV, your addiction, but that is not life. Grief is Life and so live—even with grief—so that it might accomplish its transformative work in your life.

So, Stan, read and remember, live and age, and even die gracefully by allowing the grief process to accomplish its work in you.

Yours,

28

"THE OTHER HALF OF THE STORY"

October 27, 2014

Dear Stan,

And now for the other half of the story. I have walked the journey of death too often lately but that is what happens as we age closer to our own homecoming. Diane's mother, Hazelle, lived with us for approximately three years. When she was about ninety-six years young, she began to experience "episodes," as she called them. Perhaps they were mini strokes, the doctors would not say for sure. Because all our bedrooms are on the second floor, it became too difficult for Hazelle to live with us so she moved into an adult family home nearby.

It was in October of 2012 while I was on a mission trip to Guatemala that word came to me that Hazelle had had a major "episode," was in the hospital, and was not expected to live much longer. I left the team in capable hands in Guatemala and flew home. Hazelle recovered and returned to the adult family home.

After she regained some of her capacities, I had a long conversation with her about heaven. Hazelle was a very strong believer so it was not an unusual conversation to have with her, but a few days later she told Diane about our talk and she said that she was not ready for heaven yet. She wanted to stay "here" for a while. Who was I to argue with her at age ninety-six?

But months later, when she had suffered a broken neck from a fall and the breath of life was slipping away, I again told her about heaven. Hazelle had been non-communicative for days but I rattled on, believing that she could hear me, even though there was no outward sign of recognition. At the end of my mini pep talk, Hazelle opened her eyes and said very clearly, "That's what I want," and she spoke no more.

On June 17, 2013, just one week before Diane's diagnosis of Stage IV cancer, Hazelle began the journey to a new home where there are no more tears, no more pain, no more sorrow.

So, Stan, read and remember, live and age, and even die gracefully by remembering that when the time is right, you will know. You will know when it is time to truly long for heaven.

Yours,

29

"VULNERABLE TO THE END"

October 29, 2014

Dear Stan,

Author Henri Nouwen was the first person who assisted me in seeing how a person can face his own death as the last gift given to his loved ones. I realize that my intentions at this point in my life, those intentions colored so deeply by all the experiences of the past year and a half, may not be how it will unfold in the future. Nevertheless, the following are my intentions, and I think they are positive, life-giving desires.

We all face dying differently, as a result of so many factors and variables that have influenced us on our journey. Some people face death silently, very privately. On the day of Diane's diagnosis of Stage IV cancer we decided to be open and vulnerable. We used my blog *wornsandals.com* to document our journey of the next thirteen months. By means of this online journal people in many places in our nation and in the world followed Diane's progress and our internal meanderings. Very quickly Diane found that she was not able emotionally to write, but she urged me to continue. At times I asked her permission to write about certain events, learnings, or struggles. Sometimes she said *yes* and at other times *no*.

What I learned was that people wanted and even needed to follow our journey. By our being vulnerable, others were able to open up about their pain stories. In the future, whatever God might allow to happen in my life, I want to be open and vulnerable. I want my life to be a screen, a visual image of God's faithfulness in all situations.

Sometimes when the emotional, spiritual, or even physical pain becomes too great, one might try to protect loved ones by not sharing information and even personal struggles, but I have found that this only creates more pain in others. Open communication is a true sign of love, and the flames of love need to be fanned as long as a person is physically or psychologically able.

Ultimately one faces his or her own death alone. Others cannot come on that final journey. There may come a point when it is necessary for the dying person to no longer be outwardly vulnerable but instead to go inward. When that point comes in my life, my hope and prayer are that all will have been said, all will have been done, and all those close to me will know that I love them immensely.

So, Stan, read and remember, live and age, and even die gracefully by dying vulnerably.

Yours,

30

"BEAUTY"

December 31, 2014

Dear Stan,

I arrived at Tolovana Inn, just south of Cannon Beach, Oregon, in time for a long, sunset walk. The orb of the sun had already disappeared beyond the far reaches of the Pacific Ocean, but my dog, Hanna, and I scampered down to the beach to enjoy the reds, oranges, and purples of the sunset.

By coming to Cannon Beach I am taking a risk, the risk of the pain of grief-induced memories, for this section of the Northern Oregon coast was a favorite haunting ground for Diane and me. As I write this letter I have two days and two nights yet ahead of me and I am not certain what I will experience. On the drive down I prayed my favorite prayer, written by Charles de Foucauld, who lived at the emergence of the twentieth century in the Sahara Desert of Algeria:

> Father, I abandon myself into your hands.
> Do with me whatever you will.
> Whatever you may do, I thank you.

I am ready for all, I accept all.
Let only your will be done in me,
and in all your creatures.

Into your hands I commend my spirit.
I offer it to you with all the love that is in my heart.
For I love you, Lord, and so want to give myself,
to surrender myself into your hands,
without reserve and with boundless confidence,
for you are my Father. Amen

I prayed it, not knowing what is in store, but surrendering all my experiences, and all my emotions, and all my thoughts and memories to God, believing that as my Father He would accomplish in me that which I need.

Then as soon as Hanna and I arrived we received our first gift: *BEAUTY!* The beauty of the sun-drenched sky and the shimmering of pale, orange waves quietly, softly caressing the sandy beach. The western sky was alive with the paint strokes of our Artist God. What beauty! The haystack rocks south of Tolovana Inn were silhouetted with the backlit sunset.

I enjoyed the moment by walking, breathing deeply of the cold, crisp winter air, walking and watching the evening sunset slip away. As I walked I noticed a woman with her dog. She was farther up the beach, closer to the beachfront homes that line this section of the sea. She was bundled in a winter coat and comfortable blanket as she sat and watched the ever-changing beauty of the disappearing sun. As I walked south along the beach and then much later returned north, she was still there, absorbing the beauty crafted before her. This is what I want to remember—whether I am able to walk or run or just plop down in one spot, I want to take in beauty. Beauty gives life. It renews, refreshes. Beauty is a gift from our Creator, Artistic God. Beauty can be taken for granted all too often, but I want to remember to see, feel, hear, smell, and even taste all the beauty that God gives as gifts.

In the Old Testament, Job suffered great trials and was bombarded by the insensitive advice of his three "friends." Job honestly questioned God and God's answers do not come until nearly the end of the book. Those answers pointed Job to creation and all its beauty and mystery, all its ferociousness and even its tranquility. Creation points beyond itself to the Creator. Job could be only a recipient of God's actions and he could see only the footprints of God in nature. I want to remember to see the beauty before me and to see beyond the beauty to its Artist.

So, Stan, read and remember, live and age, and even die gracefully by being open to all the beauty that punctuates daily life.

Yours,

ABOUT THE AUTHOR

STAN JACOBSON IS a pastor with over thirty-five years of experience working with small and large congregations. As a result, he has walked with numerous people through both their aging and dying processes.

He has a master's of divinity degree from Luther Seminary in St. Paul, Minnesota, and received a certificate from Presbyterian Counseling Services of Seattle, Washington, for the completion of a two-year marriage and family therapy program.

As a pastor, he has had countless pastoral counseling sessions with people going through a wide variety of life experiences—including aging and facing death.

Made in the USA
Charleston, SC
29 November 2015